M000218360

This book of prayers belongs to

_____

_____

_____

date

Praise Prayers

Compiled by
James S. Yagow

CPH
SAINT LOUIS

Good
Night

God knows our needs and has given us the gift of prayer so that we will come to Him, offering praise for His blessings.

Just as the tuck of a blanket, a hug, and a goodnight kiss reassure children of our love, praise prayers also will reassure them of God's unfailing and unconditional love made perfect through Jesus Christ, our Savior.

Use these familiar melodies to sing the prayers of praise, or simply read them together. Pray, praise, and give thanks for the touch of God's love in our lives today!

For All Your Gifts

Melody: *Westminster*

For all Your gifts,
I bow my head.
I thank You, Lord,
For I am blessed.

Evening has come,
The sun has set.
Thanks be to God,
Who gives me breath.

James S. Yagow

Be Near Me, Lord Jesus

Melody: *Away in a Manger*

Be near me, Lord Jesus;
I ask You to stay close by me
    forever,
And love me, I pray.
Bless all the dear children
In Your tender care,
And take us to heaven
To live with You there.

Unknown

Blessings from Above

Melody: *Oh, Bless the Lord, My Soul*

We thank You, loving Lord,
For blessings from above.
Bless us with safety through
    the night,
And keep us in Your love.

Unknown

God Is So Good

Melody: *God Is So Good (African Melody)*

God Is so good.
God is so good.
God is so good,
He's so good to me.

This prayer song may also be used to express different themes. Sing these or compose your own:

He cares for me …
He gives me rest …
He gives me food …
He answers prayer …
He loves me so …
He cheers my soul …

Unknown

Heavenly Father

Melody: *Jesus Loves Me, This I Know*

Heavenly Father, full of love,
Send Your blessings from
    above.
For the blessings of today,
In our hearts with thanks we
    pray.

Here, in God's circle,
Yes, in God's circle.
Here, in God's circle,
The circle of God's love.

Unknown

Lord, Keep Us Safe This Night

Melody: *Oh, Bless the Lord, My Soul*

Lord, keep us safe this night,
Secure us from our fears.
May angels guard us while
    we sleep,
Till morning light appears.

                                        Unknown

Father of Ours
in Heaven Above

Melody: *Common Doxology, Tallis' Canon*

Father of ours in heaven above,
We praise and thank You for
    Your love.
Our food, our homes,
    and all we wear
Tell us about Your loving care.

                                        Unknown

Bless Your Children

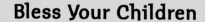

Melody: *Soul, Adorn Yourself with Gladness*

Bless Your children, Father holy,
Comfort sinners, poor and lowly.
That we serve You while we're
    living,
Health and strength to each one
    giving.
Till at last with saints we're able,
To surround Your heavenly table;
That Your blessing now
    You give us,
And throughout the night
    be with us.

Unknown

I Lift My Hands to Jesus

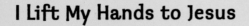

Hinky Dinky Parley Vous (French Tune)

I lift my hands to Jesus,
For He is all I need.
I lift my hands to Jesus,
For He is all I need.

He gives me food, He gives
 me drink;
He even gives me this night
 to sleep.

I lift my hands to Jesus,
For He is all I need.

Unknown

We Thank You, Lord, for Happy Hearts

Melody: *Yankee Doodle Dandy*

We thank You, Lord,
    for happy hearts,
For rain and sunny weather.
We thank You, Lord,
    for all that's good,
And that we're all together.

Thank You, thank You,
    thank You, Lord.
Thank You, Heavenly Father.
Thank You for this day
    and night,
And that we're all together.

Unknown

Great Is He!

Melody: *Three Blind Mice*

Great is He!
One yet Three.
Let God reign.
Praise His name.
Daily He gives us
    water and bread.
By His Holy Spirit
    our souls will be fed.
He gives to us life even
    though we be dead.
Oh, praise His name.

Unknown

This Day You Gave to Us

Melody: *Farmer in the Dell*

This day You gave to us,
This day You gave to us,
We thank You, oh, we thank
    You Lord,
This day You gave to us.

*Compose your own verses using the
same format. Here are some suggestions:*

Good things You give to us …
Good food You give to us …
Our home you give to us …
Your love You give to us …
A Savior You gave to us …

Unknown

For All Your Love and Happy Days

Melody: *From Heaven Above*
    to Earth I Come

For all Your love and happy days,
Accept our gratitude and praise.
In serving others, Lord, may we
Express our gratitude to Thee.

Unknown

Doxology

Melody: *Common Doxology, Tallis' Cannon*

Praise God, from whom all
    blessings flow,
Praise Him, all creatures here below.
Praise Him above, ye heav'nly host,
Praise Father, Son, and Holy Ghost.
Amen.

Public Domain

Father, We Thank You for the Night

Melody: *Common Doxology, Tallis' Canon*

Father, we thank You for
    the night,
And for the pleasant morning
    light.
For rest and food and loving care,
And all that makes the day
    so fair.

Help us to do the things
    we should,
To be to others kind and good.
In all we do in work and play,
To grow more loving every day.

Unknown

For Your Blessings

Melody: *Frère Jacques*
This prayer may be sung in a round.

For Your blessings,
      for Your blessings,
Thanks and praise,
      thanks and praise.
Joyous celebration,
      joyous celebration,
For Your ways, for Your ways.

For this day, Lord,
      for this day, Lord,
Thanks and praise,
      thanks and praise.
Joyous celebration,
      joyous celebration,
For this day, for this day.

Unknown

Accept Our Gratitude

Melody: *Common Doxology, Tallis' Canon*

Accept our gratitude,
    dear Lord,
For all the blessings You do give.
Direct and guide our daily path,
And teach us how we ought
    to live.

To God who gives us
    daily breath,
A thankful song to Him
    we'll raise,
And pray that He who gives
    us life,
Will fill our hearts with love
    and praise.

Unknown

He Lives!

Melody: *I Know That My Redeemer Lives*

He lives to bless me with
    His love;
He lives to plead for me above;
He lives my hungry soul
    to feed;
He lives to help in time of need.

He lives and grants me
    daily breath;
He lives, and I shall conquer
    death;
He lives my mansion to
    prepare;
He lives to bring me
    safely there.

Public Domain

Jesus, Tender Shepherd
Hear Me

Jesus, Tender Shepherd hear me,
Bless Your little lamb tonight;
Through the darkness please be
     near me,
Keep me safe till morning light.

All this day Your hand has led me,
And I thank You for Your care;
You have warmed and clothed
     and fed me,
Listen to my evening prayer.

May my sins be all forgiven;
Bless the friends I love so well;
Take us all at last to heaven,
Happy there with You to dwell.

Thank, Thank, Thank You!

Melody: *Row, Row, Row Your Boat*

Thank, thank, thank You, God,
Thank You now we pray.
You have given all we need
To live through every day.

Unknown

Thank You, Lord, for This Day

Melody: *Jacob's Ladder*

Thank You, Lord, for this day,
Thank You, Lord, for this day,
Thank You, Lord, for this day,
May we praise You, Lord.

Unknown

We Thank You

Melody: *Father, We Adore You*

Father, we thank You,
For Your gifts
  of blessings,
Thank You, Father.

Unknown

We Thank You for This Day

Melody: *Farmer in the Dell*

We thank You for this day,
For all Your loving care,
For sending Jesus Christ,
  our Lord.
Help us Your love to share.

Unknown

Thank You, Father Almighty

Melody: *Mary Had a Little Lamb*

Thank You,
Father Almighty,
For my friends and
    family.
Thank You, Father,
For this day,
Alleluia! Amen!

*Compose your own verses naming
things for which you are thankful.*

Unknown

T-H-A-N-K Y-O-U

Melody: *Mickey Mouse Club Jingle*

T-H-A, N-K-Y, O-U
Jesus Christ.
Thank You, Lord.
Thank You, Lord.
For all the gifts You've
given us today.
T-H-A, N-K-Y, O-U
Jesus Christ.

Unknown

May He Bless Us

Melody: *Ten Little Indians*

May He bless us as we
  slumber,
May He bless us as we
  slumber,
May He bless us as we
  slumber,
In His loving care now.

We are thanking our
  Lord Jesus,
We are thanking our
  Lord Jesus,
We are thanking our
  Lord Jesus,
For His saving love now.

Unknown

Good Morning

Promise and possibility
greet us each new
morning. With the rising
sun come new opportunities
for living another day to
God's glory, in gratitude
for His gifts of grace.

Sing, shout, or whisper
these praise prayers as you
greet each day.

Pray, praise, and give
thanks for God's protection
through the night and the
promise of His faithfulness
throughout the day!

Thank You, Lord, for This Your Day

Melody: *Michael, Row the Boat Ashore*

Thank You, Lord,
    for this Your day,
Alleluia.
Thank You, Lord,
    for this Your day,
Alleluia.

We are here to praise Your name,
Alleluia.
We are here to praise Your name,
Alleluia.

Add your own phrases for things you thank God for today.

Unknown

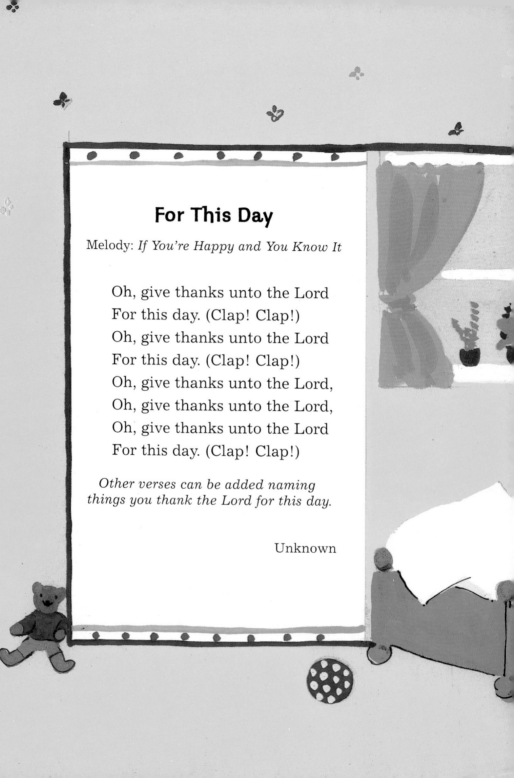

For This Day

Melody: *If You're Happy and You Know It*

Oh, give thanks unto the Lord
For this day. (Clap! Clap!)
Oh, give thanks unto the Lord
For this day. (Clap! Clap!)
Oh, give thanks unto the Lord,
Oh, give thanks unto the Lord,
Oh, give thanks unto the Lord
For this day. (Clap! Clap!)

*Other verses can be added naming
things you thank the Lord for this day.*

Unknown

God, Our Father

Melody: *Frère Jacques*
This prayer may also be sung in a round.

For Your Blessings:

> God our Father,
> God our Father,
> Once again,
> Once again,
> We will ask Your blessing,
> We will ask Your blessing,
> On this day.
> On this day.

Unknown

Thank You, God, for Peace and Rest

Melody: *Jesus Loves Me, This I Know*

Thank You, God, for peace
and rest,
And for giving us this day.
Thank You, God, for being
here,
Keeping us from every fear.

Yes, God, we love You,
Yes, God, we love You.
Yes, God, we love You,
For all Your blessings here.

Unknown

We Thank You
for the Morning Light

Melody: *Common Doxology, Tallis' Canon*

We thank You for the morning light,
For rest and shelter of the night.
For health and food, for love and
    friends,
For everything Your goodness sends.

Unknown

Lord, Lord, Give Us Strength

Melody: *Row, Row, Row Your Boat*

Lord, Lord, give us strength
And enrich our faith.
Christ is living here with us.
To guide us in our day.

Unknown

Rejoice in the Lord Always

Melody: *Rejoice in the Lord Always*
This prayer may also be sung in a round.

Rejoice in the Lord always,
And again I say, rejoice!
Rejoice in the Lord always,
And again I say, rejoice!
Rejoice! Rejoice!
And again I say, rejoice!
Rejoice! Rejoice!
And again I say, rejoice!

Public Domain

Praise Him in the Morning

Melody: *Praise Him, Praise Him*

Praise Him, praise Him.
Praise Him in the morning,
Praise Him at the noontime.
Praise Him, praise Him,
Praise Him when the sun goes
down.

Public Domain

Dearest Lord, Hear Our Praise

Melody: *This Old Man*

Dearest Lord, hear our praise,
For the joys that fill our days.
With a glad heart, praise the
Lord;
Alleluia sing. Thanks unto our
God we bring.

Unknown

Oh, Thank You, God

Melody: *America, the Beautiful*

Oh thank You, God,
    for morning time,
We start the day with You.
You give us what our bodies
    need,
And lovely weather too.
We thank You, God;
    We praise You, God;
We sing to You today.
We thank You for our freedom,
    Lord,
To praise You every day.

Unknown

Lord Jesus Christ, Be Present Now

Melody: *Common Doxology, Tallis' Canon*

Lord Jesus Christ, be present
 now;
Our hearts in true devotion
 bow.
Your Spirit send with grace
 divine,
And let Your truth within us
 shine.

All glory to the Father, Son,
And Holy Spirit, Three-in-One!
To You, O blessed Trinity,
Be praise throughout eternity!

Public Domain

Table Grace Prayers

Coming together and sharing a meal strengthens the bond of closeness. Forgiveness is ours as we gather around the table of the Lord's Supper, and memories are created around tables where food and fellowship are shared.

As you gather around your table, bring focus to the bounty of God's blessings as you lift your voices in praise.

Pray, praise, and give thanks to God for physical and spiritual nourishment, today and every day!

God, We Thank You

Melody: *Mary Had a Little Lamb*

God, we thank You for this food,
For this food, for this food.
God, we thank You for this food,
Thank You, who gives us life.

Unknown

We Thank You, Lord

Melody: *Common Doxology, Tallis' Canon*

We thank You, Lord, for this
    our food;
For daily love and daily care.
Help us to use these gifts
    of grace,
To gladly serve You everywhere.

Unknown

Bless Our Friends

Melody: *Edelweiss*

Bless our friends,
    bless our food;
Come, O Lord, and sit with us.
Make our talk glow with peace;
Come with Your love
    to surround us.
Friendship and peace may
    they bloom and grow,
Bloom and grow forever.
Bless our friends,
    bless our food;
Bless our time here together.

Unknown

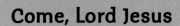

Come, Lord Jesus

Melody: *Twinkle, Twinkle Little Star*

Come, Lord Jesus, be our guest,
Let these gifts to us be blessed.
Help our bodies to be strong.
Please be with us all day long.
Come, Lord Jesus, be our guest,
Let these gifts to us be blessed.

Unknown

Great God, the Giver of All Good

Melody: *Common Doxology, Tallis' Canon*

Great God, the giver of all good,
Accept our praise and bless our food.
Grace, health, and strength
    to us afford,
Through Jesus Christ,
    our blessed Lord.

Unknown

Johnny Appleseed Song

Melody: *Traditional*

O-h, the Lord is good to me,
And so I thank the Lord,
For giving me the things I need,
The sun and the rain and
      the apple seed.
The Lord is good to me.
Amen! Amen! Amen, Amen, Amen!
A—men!

And every seed I sow,
Will grow into a tree.
And someday there'll be apples
      there
For everyone in the world to share.
The Lord is good to me.
Amen! Amen! Amen, Amen, Amen!
A—men!

Unknown

For Food You Give to Us

Melody: *Farmer in the Dell*

> For food You give to us,
> For food You give to us;
> We thank You, Lord,
> We thank You, Lord,
> For food You give to us.

Unknown

Lord Jesus, You Have Been Our Guest

Melody: *Common Doxology, Tallis' Canon*

Lord Jesus, You have been
    our guest,
We thank You for the food so blest.
Oh, may Your grace to us be given;
One day to be Your guest in
Heaven. Amen.

Unknown

Come, Lord Jesus, Be Our Guest

Melody: Frère Jacques

This prayer can be sung responsively or together as an echo.

Leader: Come, Lord Jesus.

Response: Come, Lord Jesus.

Leader: Be our guest.

Response: Be our guest.

Leader: Let these gifts to us
   be blest.

Response: Let these gifts to us
   be blest.

Leader: Amen.

Response: Amen.

Unknown

God Is Great and God Is Good

Melody: *Twinkle, Twinkle Little Star*

God is great and God is good,
And we thank Him for our food.
By His hand we all are fed,
Give us, Lord, our daily bread.
God is great and God is good,
And we thank Him for our food.

Unknown

Thanks Be to You for Friendship Shared

Melody: *Common Doxology, Tallis' Canon*

Thanks be to You for friendship
    shared,
Thanks be to You for food prepared.
Please bless this drink and bless
    this bread.
Your blessings rest upon each head.

Unknown

Special Occasions

Special occasions bring surprises and treasures, smiles and pleasures. There are many occasions that call for a celebration.

God's Son, Jesus Christ, won the victory that makes the greatest celebration of all possible—eternal life in heaven!

Pray, praise, and give thanks for today's celebration and for our forever celebration to come!

My Special Day
Is Now Here, Lord

Melody: *Take Me Out to the Ball Game*

My special day is now here,
  Lord.
Thank You, Lord, for this day.
You carried my sins upon
  Your back.
You gave me more than I'll ever
  give back.
Help me live this day to Your
  glory,
With all I do in Your name.
Father, Son, and Ho-o-ly Ghost,
Three-in-One the same. Amen.

Unknown

Traditional

There are times when our hearts are so full they spontaneously spill over into prayers of praise. And there are times when we take great comfort in praying familiar prayers and reciting familiar words.

Prayers that are familiar offer solice and comfort; much like the warmth of a hug and the touch of a hand.

Pray, praise, and give thanks that God reaches out to us through Word and Sacrament. We respond to His great love as, through prayer, we reach back to Him!

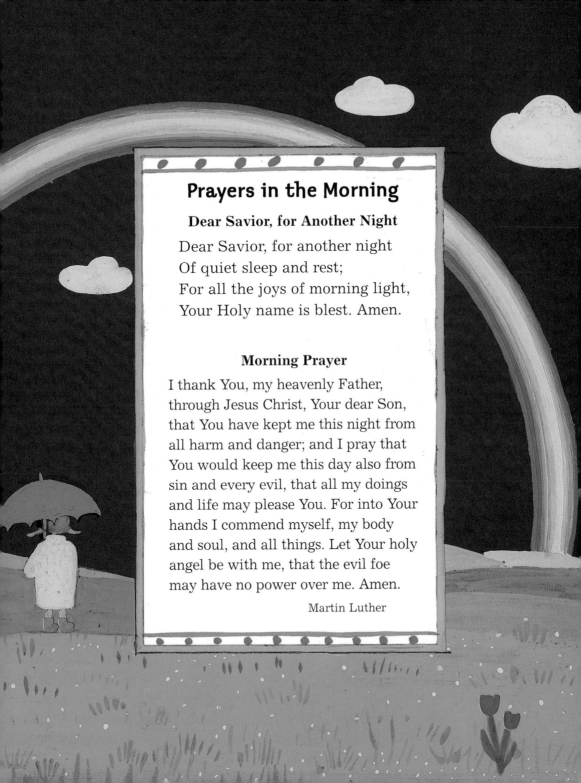

Prayers in the Morning

Dear Savior, for Another Night

Dear Savior, for another night
Of quiet sleep and rest;
For all the joys of morning light,
Your Holy name is blest. Amen.

Morning Prayer

I thank You, my heavenly Father,
through Jesus Christ, Your dear Son,
that You have kept me this night from
all harm and danger; and I pray that
You would keep me this day also from
sin and every evil, that all my doings
and life may please You. For into Your
hands I commend myself, my body
and soul, and all things. Let Your holy
angel be with me, that the evil foe
may have no power over me. Amen.

Martin Luther

Prayers at Night

Now I Lay Me Down to Sleep

Now I lay me down to sleep.
I pray You, Lord, my soul to keep.
Your love be with me through
    the night,
And wake me with the morning
    light.

Traditional

Evening Prayer

I thank You, my heavenly Father, through Jesus Christ, Your dear Son, that You have graciously kept me this day; and I pray that You would forgive me all my sins where I have done wrong, and graciously keep me this night. For into Your hands I commend myself, my body and soul, and all things. Let Your holy angel be with me, that the evil foe may have no power over me. Amen.

Martin Luther

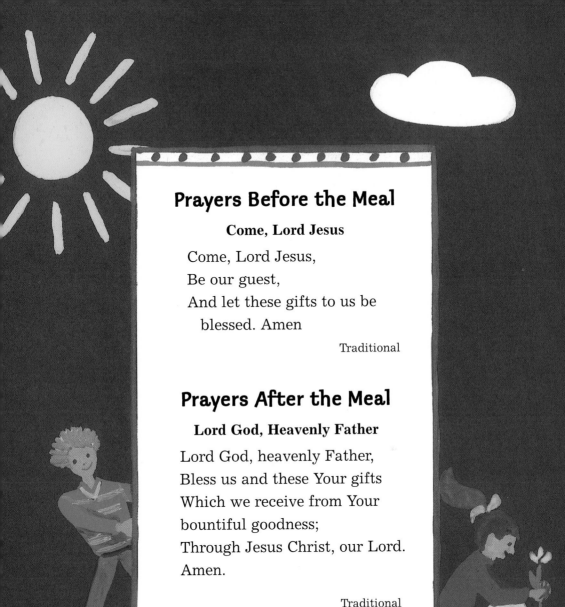

Prayers Before the Meal

Come, Lord Jesus

Come, Lord Jesus,
Be our guest,
And let these gifts to us be
    blessed. Amen

Traditional

Prayers After the Meal

Lord God, Heavenly Father

Lord God, heavenly Father,
Bless us and these Your gifts
Which we receive from Your
bountiful goodness;
Through Jesus Christ, our Lord.
Amen.

Traditional

The Lord's Prayer

Our Father who art in heaven,
Hallowed be Thy (Your) name,
Thy (Your) kingdom come,
Thy (Your) will be done
On earth as it is in heaven.
Give us this day (today)
    our daily bread.
Forgive us our trespasses (sins)
As we forgive those who trespass
    (sin) against us.
And lead us not into temptation,
But deliver us from evil.
For thine is the kingdom
    and the power and the glory
    forever and ever. Amen.

Adapted for children

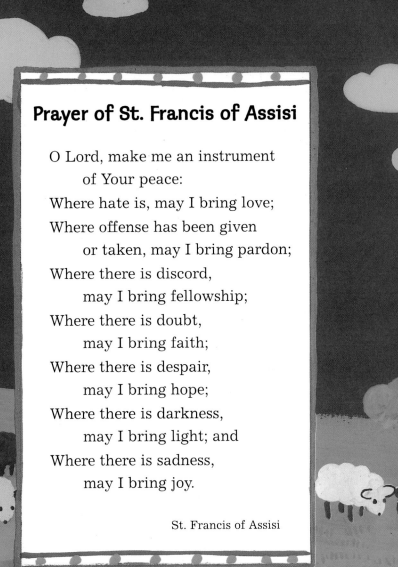

Prayer of St. Francis of Assisi

O Lord, make me an instrument
  of Your peace:
Where hate is, may I bring love;
Where offense has been given
  or taken, may I bring pardon;
Where there is discord,
  may I bring fellowship;
Where there is doubt,
  may I bring faith;
Where there is despair,
  may I bring hope;
Where there is darkness,
  may I bring light; and
Where there is sadness,
  may I bring joy.

St. Francis of Assisi

Acknowledgments

Every effort has been made to determine copyright holders of the texts included in this book. The publisher regrets any errors or oversights which may have occurred and will readily make proper acknowledgment in future editions if such omissions are made known.

The following copyrights are gratefully acknowledged:

Text: "For All Your Gifts," Copyright © 1999 James S. Yagow. Used by permission.

Text: "Jesus, Tender Shepherd Hear Me" from *Little Folded Hands*, Revised Edition. Copyright © 1959 Concordia Publishing House. Used by permission.

Text: "Morning Prayer" from *Luther's Small Catechism*. Copyright © 1986 Concordia Publishing House. Used by permission.

Text: "Evening Prayer" from *Luther's Small Catechism*. Copyright © 1986 Concordia Publishing House. Used by permission.

For reference, you can find the following melodies in most denominational hymnals and in *Lutheran Worship*, copyright © 1982 Concordia Publishing House:

Soul, Adorn Yourself with Gladness, Schmücke dich, Hymns 239, 468.

From Heaven Above to Earth I Come, Vom Himmel hoch, Hymns 37, 38.

Tallis' Canon, Hymns 254, 470, 484.

I Know That My Redeemer Lives, Duke Street, Hymns 264, 312.

Co-published in arrangement with
hanssler-Kinderland

Copyright © 1999 by
Concordia Publishing House
3558 S. Jefferson Avenue, St. Louis, MO
63118-3968

Illustrations copyright © by
Hänssler-Verlag, Germany.
Owned by assignment by Hänssler Publishing.

Manufactured in the United States of America
All rights reserved. No part of this publication
may be reproduced, stored in a retrieval system,
or transmitted, in any form or by any means,
electronic, mechanical, photocopying, recording,
or otherwise, without the prior written permission of Concordia Publishing House.

1 2 3 4 5 6 7 8 9 10   08 07 06 05 04 03 02 01 00 99